LET'S SAVE HUMANITY AND LIFE

Dr. François Adja Assemien

Copyright © 2021 Dr. François Adja Assemien.

All rights reserved. No part of this book may be reproduced in any form or by any electronic or mechanical means, including information storage and retrieval systems, without permission in writing from the publisher, except by reviewers, who may quote brief passages in a review.

ISBN: 978-1-63795-424-9 (Paperback Edition)
ISBN: 978-1-63795-425-6 (Hardcover Edition)
ISBN: 978-1-63795-423-2 (E-book Edition)

Book Ordering Information

Phone Number: 315 288-7939 ext. 1000 or 347-901-4920
Email: info@globalsummithouse.com
Global Summit House
www.globalsummithouse.com

Printed in the United States of America

Contents

From The Same Author vii
Introduction ix

1 – The Executioners 1
2 – The Slaves Of The New World Order 6
3 – The Rebels Against The New World Order 9
4 – Dialectics Of Executioners And Slaves 12
5 – Dialectics Of Executioners And Rebels 15
6 – Dialectics Of Rebels And Slaves 18
7 – Philocure Against Covid-19 22

Conclusion 37
Book Summary 41
Author's Biography 43

From The Same Author

- The African Rebels, novel, Edilivre, 2016
- African Consciousness, essay, Edilivre, 2016
- The Golden Rules of Personal Success, Happiness, Health and Salvation, Edilivre, 2016
- Introduction to philocure, essay, Edilivre, 2016
- Forbidden Africa, novel, Edilivre, 2016
- The World is worth nothing, essay, Edilivre, 2016
- Côte d'Ivoire hurts, essay, Edilivre, 2018
- The way to live in America, guide, Edilivre, 2019
- The current slavery in Africa, essay, Global Summit House, 2000
- Moral and spiritual education, manual, Edilivre, 2016
- Thomas Sankara like Thomas More and Socrates, essay, Ouagadougou, 2020
- Ahikaba, novel, Mary Bro Foundation Publishing, London, 2018
- Côte d'Ivoire with its foreigners, essay, Black Stars, 2002
- The African Guide to Philosophy, Humanities and Humanism, 1985
- Political Thought to Save Côte d'Ivoire, essay, Afro-Star, 2003
- Electoral Code, novel, Black Stars, 1995
- Portrait of the good and the bad voter, of the good and the bad candidate, essay, Black Stars, 2000
- The Eleven Evils of Côte d'Ivoire, essay, Afro-Star, 2005.

Introduction

The world and human lives are in danger. That worries me and inspires me to say and write. Events, situations, problems, crises, tragedies, dramas, scandals and catastrophes constitute my topic matter as a philosopher, sociologist, thinker, writer and humanist. These are my food for thought. I work on these things all day and night on. The story that is being made is my school. It gives me ideas and facts. As such, I greet and bless the arrival in the world of internet and social networks. These are my classrooms and my libraries. These things have effectively replaced physical books and human teachers. They are very efficient. They flood humanity with all-round knowledge and information. I feel overwhelmed and carried away by the flood of breathtaking news and knowledge that these recent inventions are pouring out into the world. Thanks to them, I realize that the world is unified and has become a single point, a very small point which no longer holds any secrets for anyone. Any event that occurs anywhere, in a distant village (town or country) is instantly known everywhere, all over the earth at the same time. Nothing can therefore be hidden in the world. And any misfortune that strikes an isolated individual (George Floyd) simultaneously affects everyone. It immediately becomes the business of the whole earth. There is no longer a local or national problem. Any problem is now international and global.

Everything and absolutely everything is shared with the whole world: pain, misfortune, pleasure, happiness, good news as well as bad news. Thus the whole earth is saying today: "I cannot breathe" or "The life of the black matters" alluding to the barbaric, very cruel assassination of the black American, George Floyd, by a white police officer with the complicity and the collaboration of his non-black colleagues.

The whole earth suffers from the damage and horrors of corona virus at the same time (death of people, confinement, wearing of face masks, physical distance, tele-work, tele-education, paranoia, panic…). Globalization (or the New World Order) affects everyone. Earth is truly unified, dominated, exploited and tyrannically ruled by a capitalist and predatory oligarchy (mafia). This international oligarchy is globalist, eugenicist, satanist, freemasonic. They created corona virus (global chaos) and sowed the panic that they exploits for their hegemonic, geopolitical, geo-economic, geo-cultural, geo-philosophical and geo-ideological ends. Before this class of executioners (predatory lions) are the slaves class and the rebels class. So the present world is made up of three categories of people forming a triangle or a trilogy. It is the Human Triangle (executioners, slaves, rebels). You, who read this book, you are in which category? Are you an executioner (oligarch, lion, predator), a slave (sheep), a rebel (resistant, disobedient)?

Be human and responsible. We are at war. Take a stand. Choose your side. This time is very serious. No one has the right to be neutral, impartial, indifferent, insensitive, oblivious, reckless and irresponsible. Everyone must absolutely define himself, determine himself, know himself, situate himself, choose his status and his fight. It is a matter of life or death. If you want to live, you have to fight, defend yourself and improve your situation. It is a question of remaking history of humanity in justice, for the good, the happiness and the salvation of all. So this book is mainly intended for sheep or lion prey. The time for revolutionary engagement has come.

1
The Executioners

Who are the executioners of humanity? How far does their degree of nuisance or malfeasance extend? What are their relationships with the slaves and the rebels they created? The executioners revealed by the shattering arrival of covid-19 in the world are the masters, the powerful, the rulers who control earth geopolitically, geo-economically, geo-culturally, geo-ideologically, geo-scientifically, geo-philosophically and militarily. They form an oligarchic class and practice terrorism, dictatorship and mafia predation everywhere on earth. They enslaved, colonized peoples in Asia, Europe, Africa, America and Oceania. They continue to enslave and colonize Africans, Europeans, Americans, Asians and Oceanians. They massacre and exterminate with impunity and without moral scruple entire peoples in the world. This is how they created colonies (concentration camps or colonial empires) on all continents which they dominate and exploit to satiety and cheerfully without embarrassment or modesty. They sow terror, misery, desolation and humanitarian catastrophe as well as natural calamities wherever they set foot.

They imposed an order on the whole world. This order is political, economic, social, moral, legal, philosophical, religious, cultural, civilizational, ideological. We owe them everything in their dominant culture-civilization. Everything belongs to them. All activities of this world benefit them. All the peoples on earth are working for them, for their enrichment. Sometimes they hide themselves and use cunning and violence. They do a lot of harm in the shadows, under angelic appearances. They manipulate, instrumentalize, abuse all humans by a system called the **world order**. Their covid-19 arrived as a volcanic eruption that suddenly brings out the incadescent magma that is ravaging everything. It is the execution of a devilish plan plotted by the executioners for centuries for the establishment of a **catastrophic new world order**. The latter want to go further in their cynicism, their diabolicity and their cruelty. It wakes people up. Humans are opening their eyes. They seek to know and understand the foundation of the world order, of the value system. Covid-19 is then what brings to light what is hidden behind the curtain and the veil of the controllers, the dominators and the masters of the world (the executioners). Covid-19 is the offshoot of the devastating magma that is the creation of a new world order as a strengthening of the usual world order or the profound transformation by the destruction of the world, the slaughter of 80% of the inhabitants of earth and zombification- robotization of 20%. It's quite a satanic program. Covid-19 is the concrete start of this macabre project of the globalists. It opens the door for us to a new civilization that is being imposed on us by war ("We are at war", according to President Emmanuel Macron). Covid-19 is an instrument of the globalizing executioners, a boulevard that leads the world straight to hell. And its taste, being very bitter and unbearable, wakes us from our too deep sleep. Because it is synonymous with eugenics, racism, genocide, hecatomb, apocalypse, terrorism, that is to say massacre on a planetary scale, on human, social, economic, cultural, political, religious, ideological, philosophical levels.

The present time is for the creation of a new world order. It is not a democratic action. It is an act of barbarism, a secret, hypocritical war waged by the world elite dominating all States and all world governments against the peoples. The creation of a new world order is not a consensual action of the states and peoples on earth. It is happening above the heads of governments and peoples. This is happening secretly without the knowledge of all States and all peoples. It is a top secret matter, a conspiracy of the international business elite who own or operate the pharmaceutical, food, and biochemical industries around the world. This business elite is now turned towards frenzied control, drastic reduction and compulsory vaccination of the world population. They are in a satanic utopia inspired by an implacable thirst for power, control, domination, the digitization of men thanks to compulsory vaccination which will inoculate an electronic chip in the body of every person on earth. This utopia aims to sterilize women, to kill as many people as possible, to depopulate earth. It wants to wipe out 80% of the world's population and keep only 20%. These 20% of the population will constitute guinea pigs or subjects of all-out scientific experimentation. Humans will be transformed into zombies or sheep totally submissive and obedient to order, to a tyrannical, dynastic, castic collectivist system. Robots and computers will do everything instead of men. It will be the absolute triumph of science, technology, technocracy, geoengineering. Physical currency will be phased out in favor of digital currency. The whole economy and all political, social and cultural life will be digitized and mechanized. It is the era of artificial intelligence. This is already (or since) being tested in the world and it works wonderfully, devilishly. The digitization of the world is the outrageous industrialization, the exaggerated mechanization and technicalization of the world and of human life. We are in the midst of delirious utopianism and scientism. We are in planetary mortal madness. Scientists and scholars will have all the powers and the right of life or death over everyone. They alone will do everything. They will reign over everyone's life. Through them, eugenics, globalists, globalizers, governments, and the satanic and business elite spread deadly poisons into the air, into the atmosphere and kill millions of people. It's officially called covid-19. It is the spreading of toxic products such as aluminum, sulfur dioxide, hydrogen sulphate, excessive radio-electric radiations of 5 G (ultra high frequency). To this, the executioners add the RFID chip. And the blow is played. It is robbery, terrorism to the absolute degree and criminality never equaled in human history because it is against all humanity and universal civilization at the same time. The perpetrators of this supreme crime are Bill and Melinda Gates, the Bilderberg Club, WHO, GAVI, GSK, Rothschild Foundation, Rockefeller Foundation, Big pharma ...

The latter blithely violate the rules of bioethics or international ethics. They have biological weapons. They use them against the world population in the realization of their eugenics. They push the daring to the creation of human beings through cloning, artificial insemination. They seek to create a tyrannical, dynastic world government with representatives from five continents and a digital global currency. They corrupt, alienate and use all the influential people in this world (political and religious leaders, high military hierarchy, businessmen, journalists, scientists, scientists, doctors ...). Their representatives and defenders are present everywhere and are very dynamic. They are doing everything to submit and prevent the world's populations from rising up against them. They keep them in total ignorance of their world plot. So people cannot suspect their innumerable and catastrophic crimes nor believe that this can exist. Whistleblowers are ridiculed and called conspirationnists. They are seen as crazy and delusional paranoid. The executioners have infiltrated and recovered all socio-human, socio-political, socio-economic, socio-cultural and socio-spiritual environments. They want to impose a religion, theirs, on the whole earth or on all the peoples tamed, colonized, unified, enslaved by them. This is Satanism or free masonry (the Illuminati).

They will suppress all other existing religions (Judeo-Christianity, Islam, Buddhism, Hinduism...). They will form a very powerful and formidable universal army. It will be like NATO but very strengthened and over-equipped for the needs of the new world order.

2

The Slaves Of The New World Order

Who are the slaves of the new world order? It is all those who are passive in front of the phenomenon of corona virus. These are all people in the world who endure the corona virus conspiracy without complaining, revolting or resisting the realization of the new world order. They are the resigned victims, that is to say, people who are mistreated, dominated, submissive, obedient. These are people who do not oppose the global covid-19 scam, who do not fight, doubt, question the nature, origin, manifestations, causes, consequences of covid-19. They are the blessed yes, yes. Slaves are all "sleepers", all "dumb" and all those who do not defend themselves.

Why are they like this? They are so for very diverse and multiple reasons. For example, ignorance, fear, cowardice, stupidity, unconsciousness, recklessness, indifference. Among the world's 17 billion people, there are very few people who are educated, informed, learned. Very few people are literate and able to follow and understand world news, history, events and issues. Very few people care about what is happening on earth. Even among the official intellectuals, or the educated, cultured people with the means and the capacity to inform themselves, to follow and to understand the phenomenon of covid-19, there are many slaves.

Sheep are, alas, among all strata of the world's population. It all depends on each person's personality, on his situation, relationships with others or his condition of life. It is not a matter of diplomas or social rank. Humans are subject to various and multiple influences from everywhere (State, family, profession, press, church, temple, mosque, street, club, association, army, public opinion...). Most people are acted, manipulated, corrupted, robotic. They don't think by themselves. They don't think. They are not critical, skeptical, responsible. They allow themselves to be poisoned and easily manipulated by rumors, prejudices, lies and behave like Panurge sheep. They have not developed resistance capacities in them to be able to defend and protect themselves. So they can be manipulated at will. They are at the mercy of everyone. They have no will or reason. They are weak in character regardless of their level of education, culture and learning. But the vast majority of slaves belong to the ignorant class.

Fear and cowardice also make slaves and sheep. There are people who are fearful and cowardly by nature. They are found in all segments of the world's population. Regardless of their rank or social status. They are weaklings. They are light-hearted, irresponsible. They never dare to act or react against global issues like covid-19. They are afraid. They believe that they will die if they do not obey the barrier measures dictatorially imposed on them by their torturers. They fear being punished by the same torturers. They support the macabre system. They are corrupt and alienated. They are in the pay of their executioners. They are stubborn and dumb. You can explain things to them rationally and objectively, with supporting evidence, but they continue to be afraid, to tremble and to obey. They refuse to understand things. They prefer to obey the criminal injunctions of the executioners. They make it too easy for the assassins. They are the most numerous. It is the herd made up of guinea pigs and sacrificial sheep. They are expiatory animals deprived of common sense, intelligence and Reason. They live in emotion (fear, dread). Reason is for the executioner and emotion is for the slave. The slave obediently accepted his confinement, physical distancing and wearing face masks believing that it may save him from danger of death. He is gullible, naive and imbecile.

Moreover, the slave is not concerned about what is happening in the world. He is not aware of the dangers or the gravity of the present situation. He is not concerned about global health problems. It ignores the phenomenon of the new world order. He lives in a way in indifference, like a child. He has a childish mind. He is insensitive, passive, blinded. He is guided by his enemies, the executioners. He does not believe in the scientific truth which is provided by the whistleblowers. He is only nourished by the illusions, lies, prejudices and rumors of vulgar people. Public opinion is enough for him. That is his faith and his absolute truth.

3

The Rebels Against The New World Order

Who are the rebels against the new world order? They are people like us, that is to say rebellious men and women, fighters, critics. They are awake. They are intellectual, scientific, political, social, economic, cultural, spiritual fighters. They are strategists and tacticians. The rebels are all resistants to the world order which is on the march. They are people who call on others to resist and disobey the macabre, criminal value system. Rebels are all those who think, reflect, criticize, judge and condemn endless crimes and unbearable, hellish, apocalyptic evil. They are all the brave, courageous, martyrs and heroes who find that the world is in danger and that what is happening right now is very unfair, very abnormal, diabolical, demonic, satanic. The rebels are awakened people who are fighting to protect, defend and save humanity from the crimes of depopulation of the earth, of eugenics, neo-colonialism and the capitalist oligarchy. They are those who have decided to fight and sacrifice themselves for the benefit of others, that is to say, the blind, the ignorant, the sheep, the slaves. The rebels represent a handful of enlightened and honest people on earth who are not manipulable. They are bones in the throats of bandits, terrorists, criminals, brigands, mafiosi who manipulate all of humanity. The rebels are rebellious, angry, furious. They are insurgents and "warriors". They are not cowardly. They dare to denounce, stigmatize and incriminate globalists, eugenics, point the finger at executioners such as Bill and Melinda Gates, the Bilderberg Club, WHO, Jacques Attali, Georges Soros, Rothschild, Rockefeller. They dare to denounce the supreme dangers of geoengineering, microbiology, 5 G, murderous spraying, the secret war against peoples, compulsory vaccinations, the electronic chip controlling all humans, the single digital currency project. They denounce them as they are dangerous as the plans to create a single government collectivist, dynastic, barbaric, criminal, a global single religion, a single global language. They also condemn the projects of artificial intelligence, of suppressing 80% of the world population, of robotics, human cloning, of creating zombies and of scientism (absolute or totalitarian power of science).

The rebels are all the whistleblowers, all the humanists and all the public moralizers who denounce the lies and the plots of States. The greatest figures, figureheads and heroes among the rebels are Claire Séverac (The Secret War Against Peoples), Jean-Dominique Michel (Anatomy of a Health Crisis), Pierre Hillard and HG Wells (Le Nouvel Ordre Mondial)), Mwazulu Diyabanza, Lise Manzambi, Jérome Munyangi, Andry Rajoelina, Dr Vangu Lutete, Elianne Nkolo, Dr Emma Djinhs, Jean-Jacques Crevecoeur, Chloe F., Luc Michel, Mohamed Diallo and many others. By their number, they are inferior to the slaves we have already described in this book. The rebels are absolutely insignificant in number on earth. They are even a few drops of ocean water that constitutes the world's population. But they are very active and fearless. They block, delay, sabotage and thwart the traps of the globalists, eugenics and utopians. They defeat the catastrophic and apocalyptic plots of the latter so far. It is thanks to the rebels that we still live on earth. It is therefore thanks to their heroic struggle that earth has not yet lost 80% of its population that the eugenic globalists are keen to kill by all means (food, electricity, drugs, vaccines, drinking water, spraying, war ...). They unveil the plans of the executioners' macabre and satanic plots and force these executioners to use Machiavellian or diplomatic cunning. Under their pressure and under their constant denunciations, the executioners lie and allege that they are doing us good while massacring us (massacre, genocide). Thus they mask, veil their malfeasance, their crimes. They employ corruption, blackmail and threats in every country in the world (assassinations of resistant, honest, virtuous, human, patriotic, nationalist, revolutionary Presidents). The executioners sow confusion, doubt and terror in all hearts and minds. This makes the work of the rebels, awareness raising and whistleblowers very difficult. So no leader in this world frankly and courageously recognizes that there is this planetary war against the peoples and corona virus (covid-19) is a conspiracy, a masquerade, a lie and a system of domination, submission, exploitation, robbery, depopulation of earthe (terrorism). All political leaders are silent, accomplices, guilty. They are manipulated, dominated, corrupted, used, shameful and criminal, except the President of Madagascar, Mr. Andry Rajoelina, who stands up to the executioners. He is a powerful rebel who refuses to deliver his country and his people to the executioners. He even dared to have his own drug against covid-19 manufactured at home. What could be more normal, more just, more worthy, more reasonable, more courageous, more beautiful, more legitimate, more responsible on the part of an African President? He openly fights the WHO and the whole corrupting and criminal system of executioners. He rejects all their satanic injunctions. He wants to be independent, sovereign. He is very vigilant and careful. He personally watches over the health, safety and well-being of his people. He is loyal to his country. He is responsible and dignified. He thus moralizes all the Presidents of the world. The other African Presidents would benefit from imitating him.

4

Dialectics Of Executioners And Slaves

Can a slave turn into an executioner? And can an executioner become a slave? Is there a dialectic between these two categories of individuals? The executioner is wicked. The slave is his victim. If the executioner is a lion, the slave is a sheep. Can the lion take the place of the sheep and the sheep the place of the lion? The lion's nature is fixed, stable, permanent. It is fixed forever. It's closed, finished. A lion is born and remains a lion. He dies a lion. Leonity is irreducible, unchangeable. It cannot be transformed. Leonity is power. It cannot become weakness. The lion only knows how to kill and devour his prey. If he stops doing this, he will starve to death. So he cannot be transformed into a sheep, that is to say into his prey. The lion was born to devour weak animals, to dominate them. He's an eternal king.

This is not the case with the sheep, that is to say with the slave. The slave is weak. Bondage is weakness. But it's a weakness that can evolve. It can become a force under certain conditions. As a human being, the slave is endowed with Reason, intelligence, conscience and will. He can think and reflect on his fate. He can judge his master, his executioner and condemn him. He can complain and revolt against the wickedness of his executioner. He can decide to

Dialectics Of Executioners And Slaves

free himself from bondage and fight this injustice. It is said that fear made the first slaves and that their cowardice kept them in bondage. But if they let go of their fear, their cowardice, and decide to fight against their masters, they change their destiny, their fate and their life. They manage to defeat their tormentors and free themselves. This is what history teaches us. No one can endure the injustice, oppression, domination, suffering, violence of others indefinitely. In this sense, J.-J. Rousseau said: "The strongest is never strong enough to always be the master if he does not transform his strength into right and obedience into duty". Thus the frustrations, violence and prolonged injustices in some societies have engendered anger, revolt and acts of revenge. In capitalist societies, injustice, oppression and cynical exploitation of workers by bourgeois employers have provoked the revolution of the proletarians and the fall of bourgeois, capitalist regimes.

We went from capitalist liberalism to socialism and communism. Thus the dictatorship of the bourgeoisie entails the dictatorship of the proletariat and the communist society. It is the dialectic of the bourgeoisie and the proletariat. The appeal launched by Karl Marx to the proletarians did not fall on deaf ears: "Workers of all countries, unite". This indeed had its revolutionary effect. This call changed the face of the world. France, for example, has made several revolutions. It passed from the absolute monarchy of divine right to the republic. Kings or executioners have been massacred, executed by their victims in revolt and united in the struggle. Sheep can therefore become lions. They can do justice to themselves. This is possible when they have historical and political awareness, when they manifest their Reason and their will. "Reason decides what is right and anger wants us to find just what Reason has decided". The real strength or the greatest power is found among the people, that is to say, among the slaves of circumstance. Sovereignty belongs to the people and to each person. This is inalienable. You just have to be brave and want to exercise it. All people are born free, equal in rights and in dignity. Servitude or slavery is a historical accident, a fact of life. It is neither essential nor eternal. Unless the slave denies his nature, his freedom, his sovereignty, his will. No one should accept that someone else decides his fate or anything for him. No one should accept that his freedom, his life, his sovereignty, his natural and civil rights are stolen. Everyone must demand, with all his might, absolute respect for his rights by those in power and everyone: right to life, right to health, right to security, right to liberty, right to happiness, right to work , right to movement, right to expression ...

5

Dialectics Of Executioners And Rebels

The role of the executioners is to annihilate the rebels or, at the very least, to silence them. The executioners want to dominate and control all men on earth. They are terrorists and dictators who do not accept to see someone resist them or escape them. They are determined to go to the end of their satanic adventure. So they do not hesitate to use all the means likely to assure them victory. They proceed through assassinations, corruption and all kinds of violence. They control and subdue all the rulers of the world. All influential men on earth, all commercial and industrial companies and all international institutions are at their service and at their command. They rule the whole earth.

The rebels represent nothing to them as strength or power. The rebels are only a small group of discreet people, without means, without defense, without force. They act in the shadows, in secret. As soon as they are displayed or revealed, they are subdued and murdered (Claire Séverac, Bob Marley). They publish books and post videos on social media. They express themselves through private televisions, not corrupted or controlled by corrupted states. There is, for example, Afrique Média TV, a pan-Africanist television station based in the Cameroon which gives voice to African rebels like Dr. Emma Djinhs, Banda Kani, Dr Jérôme Munyangi, Luc Michel, among many others. Acting according to their methods and strategies, the rebels want to overthrow the executioners or make them fail. They are incorruptible, uncontrollable and very critical. They are sagacious, vigilant, skeptical towards official speeches, governments, media propaganda of executioners, international institutions (WHO,UN, Foundations, NATO, WB, IMF, European Union, African Union, ECOWAS etc.). They are not distracted. They do not allow themselves to be lulled to sleep nor to be caressed by the executioners and their resigned and docile servants.

The rebels have a dream: to succeed in mobilizing and transforming a very large number of slaves into rebels in order to increase their rank. They seek to widen their circle, to enlarge their group and thus to give themselves more strength and power. Because they know that the great number, the union and the solidarity make strength, victory, salvation, security and happiness of each and every one. They know that the revolutionary action of the peoples or the popular masses is irresistible and formidable. It is the instrument which has enabled Marxist-Leninists and Maoists to overcome the capitalist bourgeoisie in the class struggle. This story is school. Strength and power are with the people. They belong to people who are conscious, united, awakened, organized, courageous, brave, intrepid, fighting, responsible and worthy. Marxism-Leninism is a school here. It is the best ideological, political and historical reference. Rebels can happily draw experiences, lessons and inspiration from this powerful universal school.

The rebels want to win the greatest war in history, after the war or bourgeoisie-proletariat duality. This new war is the most difficult and the most dangerous. It spares no one on earth. If it is won by the executioners, it will be the end of humanity (Emmanuel Macron and others want to make humans-animals, zombies and human-machines). It will be the worst disaster ever known in history as the total suppression of the natural human species and the complete destruction of earth through science and technology. It is a war which is being waged with the help of chemistry, biology, bacteriology. It also uses electronics. Computing and geoengineering (spreading poisons in the atmosphere by the armies of executioners). This spawned corona virus or covid-19 as a blatant manifestation and result of the criminal and satanic policies of the West and Asia. This war can be won by the rebels with the help of the awakened slaves (popular masses) as in the days of Karl Marx, Lenin and Mao tse-Tung. Especially if the rebels infiltrate the executioners, seize their spirit and transform them into saints, virtuous people, by taking them out of their eugenic utopia (Thomas More), out of their satanic, globalist, Malthusian, Platonic ideology etc.

6

Dialectics Of Rebels And Slaves

The rebels are the mortal enemies of executioners and friends of slaves. Rebels are all those who want to prevent the executioners from achieving their macabre objectives on earth. They are heroes and martyrs who protect earth. They want to save all the peoples, all the slaves, all the goods and all the riches of earth. They fiercely fight against the influences and harmful actions of the torturers. They want to secure everyone against the new world order of executioners. They defend the slaves who are being manipulated and led underhand and hypocritically to the slaughterhouse called the New World Order. At the same time as they fight the executioners, the rebels act on the slaves. Indeed, they want to open their eyes to slaves. They seek to enlighten them, guide them and make them responsible. As Karl Marx did to the proletarians around the world, the rebels ask the slaves to open their eyes, to stand up and to fight against the executioners and their system. They reveal to them the evil plans and traps of the executioners. These are horrible things like vaccines, drugs, food, 5G, microchip, digital single currency, climate change, wearing face masks, physical distance, confinement, screening, mass murder, organ trafficking...

Dialectics Of Rebels And Slaves

In fact, the rebels inform and train the slaves. They teach them to gradually become rebels. They want to turn them into rebels, increase their strength and multiply their strength. They want to create a sacred union, very strong, united and fighting. They want to mobilize all the slaves who constitute a great unconscious, ignorant and passive force. Karl Marx pulled off this coup with the proletarians around the world. He turned them into the world's greatest, historic transformative force. He gave them moral conscience, political conscience, social conscience, economic conscience and historical conscience. He transformed and changed history. He thus created the most powerful active and revolutionary force on earth, which is the dictatorship of the proletariat. That toppled and defeated the dictatorship of the capitalist bourgeoisie. The order of the world has changed. The peoples have found freedom, peace, security, well-being, dignity. "The strongest is never strong enough to always be the master if he does not transform his strength into law and obedience into duty," said J.-J. Rousseau. The injustice, arbitrariness, cynicism and domination practiced by the minority over the majority in the world have always resulted in the violent change of order. Because it is frustrating and revolting.

What the rebels are looking for is that each people have the freedom and the right to self-determine, to self-govern, to choose his own political model, his economic model, his social model, his cultural model. Everyone must be able to live in his own civilization, according to his own paradigm. The relationship of master to slave, from bourgeois to proletarian, from executioner to victim, from globalizer to globalized must end. It must be done away with forever. From now on each individual must be free, sovereign. Each people must be free, autonomous, sovereign. The world is multiple, plural. **Everyone must create his own order**. No one has the right to impose his order on others and, even less, on the whole earth. This criminal arbitrariness is unacceptable. What will Westerners say and do if one day Africans, for example, want to impose an order on them and exterminate them like the Whites have always done and for centuries to Africans? Will they accept that? Will they find it normal, legitimate, fair, reasonable? Surely not. So why do they do it cheerfully, without batting an eyelid, to other peoples? There is a saying: "Don't do to others what you don't want them to do to you". There is a need for justice and equality among humans and peoples. Is it because the whites believe they are the strongest, the most powerful that they always do the evil to all the other peoples in the world ? Are they forgetting Rousseau's sentence which says: "The strongest is never strong enough to always be the master if he does not transform his strength into right and obedience into duty"? The sheep does not have the habit of biting people. But if one does not care too much of it by introducing at any time his finger in its mouth, it finished to bite this provocative finger. It is African folk wisdom that says so. This is true. Any excess is harmful. Any exaggeration is harmful. It is reckless. It's a risk. The West is an accident, said Roger Garaudy, a contemporary French philosopher. The latter teaches us that the West did not bring anything good, significant, essential in the creation of civilization. What the West can do (better than all other peoples) is **evil** , imperialist wars, predations, theft, looting of other peoples' goods, lies, robberies. The West is the world champion in evil and dishonesty. Read the Black Code, the Charter of Imperialism, the Colonial Pact. Think of the slave trade, colonization, the massacres of Africans, asians and native americans are there. Is that glorious ? Read Roger Garaudy in his books entitled "Call to the Livings", "The Alternative", "Dialogue of Civilizations", "Biography of the 21st Century". He establishes the truth about the nature and worth of Western and non-Western peoples. He gives the advantage to Non-Westerners, Africans and Asians. He loudly asserts that wisdom belongs to Africans and to Asians. He thinks that knowledge and civilization belong to Africans. He attributes barbarism, murderous madness and absolute ignorance to the Westerners. He is right. He is objective, honest. Indeed, he studied and compared Eastern, Western and African cultures. He is wise. What will he say yet if he lives now and he learnes that his white brothers want to destroy civilization and want to kill 80% of the global population? What will he say about the apocalyptic plot of eugenics and anti-human globalists today? What will he say about covid-19 and all that is behind this global tragedy ? What will he say about Macron, Bill and Melinda Gates and others who want to turn humans into zombies, animals, robots, suppress sex between men and women and ban natural procreation etc.?

7

Philocure Against Covid-19

Covid-19 is presented to the world as a very deadly pandemic. Its "victims" would number in the hundreds and thousands in each country. It is growing exponentially. Tomorrow it will be millions or billions victims of Covid-19 in the world. Sacred pandemic! We do not wish it. Are people really dying from covid-19 or are they dying from other diseases that have been substituted for covid-19? Some say people die with covid-19 and not from covid-19. The controversy on this issue is in full swing. Where is the truth? Beyond illness and death, there are the very serious social problems created by compulsory and general confinement almost everywhere in the world. People are ordered to stay locked up, like prisoners, at home, not to go out, not to travel, not to work. They are suddenly unemployed. And, as we know, unemployment means deprivation of wages and money. Who does not work is not paid. Idleness and unemployment lead to misery, poverty and famine. An ordinary family that no longer has any financial income cannot meet its daily expenses and basic needs such as housing, food, medical care, electricity, running water, etc.

Covid-19 has also resulted in the forced abandonment of our common, general, customs. This constitutes the killing of the current universal civilization, that is to say all of our ways of thinking, living and acting. The world is changing very rapidly before our eyes. We are overwhelmed and out of step. We are already, in just a few months, in a new world as if transported to another planet with very strange habits. Earth is no longer the land we knew only a few months ago. Everyone suddenly became very weird, strange, suspicious, fearful. All faces are now hidden. All hands are gloved. People keep their distance from each other. No more physical contact or trust between humans. Everywhere, it is necessary to avoid promiscuity, the gathering of men, crowds. It is essential to observe social distance. Everyone considers his neighbor as very dangerous or as a deadly poison that he must avoid at all costs, in the name of life. Everyone is suspect in everyone's eyes. We are now in a world of generalized suspicion where everyone is thought to be a carrier of corona virus, the supreme danger, the most frightening monster that would seek to devour everyone. Incredible but true. A whole nightmare, a whole human stupidity. It is general madness. This is the global lie. It is the universal illusion. It is also the new world fashion.

Covid-19 shows us a lot of amazing things. It shows us the strengths and weaknesses of humanity. Thanks to it, we discover the real world and the deceptive world, appearance and reality. Thus we know today that the Western countries considered formerly as super-powers are very vulnerable and very fragile. This aspect is really very surprising. It only took a few days and a few weeks of the global health and security crisis to see the entire West crumble like a paper castle. Socio-economically, the West is totally weakened or flattened. It is the descent into hell. It's a catastrophe. The West is running out of steam. He is decadent, dying. Its super-power is therefore a myth, an illusion, a deception, a fiction, a hoax. It's window dressing. It is vanity. The West is a house of cards.

We thus learn that insecurity and fear can cause the fall or the ruin of economically, politically, technically and scientifically powerful countries like the USA, Canada, France, Italy, Spain ...).

Such is the power and the value of universalized fear and lie. The universalized biggest fear and universalized biggest lie are our worst enemies and weapons of mass destruction. They are atomic and nuclear bombs in other forms. They are also very effective instruments of blackmail that help people get whatever they want. This makes it possible to transform all the inhabitants of earth into sheep to be sacrificed on the altar of madness and megalomania of a few clever, cunning and criminal individuals (those who benefit from covid-19) practicing satanism.

Covid-19 will also have taught us that all the peoples, all the inhabitants of earth are unified, united and form a single family or a single large village. Human society is an organic unit. What affects one country affects at the same time all the other countries in the world. Covid-19, manufactured by the Institut Pasteur, which holds the patent, is said to have started to show its effects in China. And in a few days, or weeks, it took over the whole world. The same behaviors can be observed simultaneously almost everywhere on earth.

Another lesson to be learned is the human capacity to transform, to adapt quickly to a new situation, to create a new way of life. This is fascinating. We see that in a few days, a few weeks or just a few months, the Asian man, the European man, the American man and the African man created all the means necessary for the life of the era of covid-19. A new civilization is on the march in the world. It replaces the civilization in which we grew up and evolved until January 2020. Habits, mentalities and human behavior are changing. History is turned upside down. It is dizzying and saddening. Man can live without using buses, boats, planes or any form of public transport. Man can be confined to his home, without having physical contact with his fellows, respecting a "social distance", wearing a mask on his face, hiding his nose, his mouth, and having gloved hands. Man can work remotely using computer, internet and smart phone. So he can study remotely, far from classrooms. We are in the civilization of tele-work, of tele-education, of tele-training, of tele-existence. We can even live without working (confinement requires) and governments that are globalizers or supporters of the New World Order plot will provide us with free food and money as compensation for the confinement they have imposed. Is life thus more beautiful and easier? Is this a dignified, responsible, happy life? Is this the ideal life for human beings? No. Not at all. This is what the Illuminati, the Freemasons and other satanic, maniacal and brainless globalists and eugenics who rule the world want to lead humanity towards. According to the Bible, God, the creator of the world and of all things, said: "Man, you will earn your bread by the sweat of your brow. Woman, you will give birth in pain "(Original Sin).

Their demonic plan aims to suppress six billion people currently living in the world and to keep only one billion people on earth that they will manage, dominate, enslave, colonize (sheep, robots, zombies). Ah Globalization! Ah new world order! This new world order imposed on all humanity by force, war, violence, barbarism, clearly shows that there is a "White-Yellow peril". It manifests the supreme degree of cruelty, folly and nuisance of the white and yellow peoples in the world. It also shows the infinite nuisance capacity of their science, their technology, their philosophy, their computing. These are physics, chemistry, biology, bacteriology, virology, climatology, ecology, economics, eugenics, Malthusianism, capitalism. This proves that the end of humanity is possible. And this end of humanity can come from eugenic, globalizing, hegemonic, belligerent, Malthusianist and satanic policies. Everything is now clear and very clear for everyone. The enemies of the world, of humanity are known.

Time is desperate. People we see around us and hear everywhere, across the world, display utter despair. They are all very confused, overwhelmed and in total disarray. Everyone is confused. People are confined, imprisoned implicitly. They are alienated, enslaved. They have lost all their fundamental rights and freedoms. They are fed and kept alive by rumors, prejudices, lies and catastrophic news that rob them of all hope and teach them their new living conditions or their new terrifying fate in this world. Everywhere it is alarmism and media hype. They are taught that they can contract covid-19 anywhere and die at any time hence generalized paranoia. Everyone must understand that he is no longer entitled to life, normal health, safety, well-being, and that he is doomed to the most atrocious and artificial death willed and caused by demons and the white satans of this world. Everyone should know that he will one day be separated from his loved ones, his parents, his family and isolated to die because he is declared infected with covid-19. Right or wrong. Everyone knows that he is exposed (defenseless) to mafia abuses of State and international terrorist organizations, mercantilists, which kill people with vaccines-poisons and other means. Everyone knows or should know that his body and organs are wanted by brigands and official assassins to save other people and that for this purpose he can be trapped and killed in hospital. Everyone should also know that sooner or later he will receive an electronic chip in his body to become sheep, guinea pig, zombie, robot, controllable wherever he is and at any time. All of this keeps the whole world in despair and panic.

This is where we will present **philocure** (our medical creation, our therapy) and its absolute usefulness or effectiveness against covid-19. If you look at our work entitled **Moral and Spiritual Education** (sold by Edilivre in France), you will find all the recipes, all strategies and the necessary remedies to combat Covid-19 and preserve your health. Indeed, covid-19 is mental poisoning. It is manipulation, psychological torture. It gives people illusion, fear, despair, feeling of helplessness, anger, discouragement, disappointment, disgust with life, mistrust, pessimism, angst, frustration, dread. Covid-19 is a web of traumatic and deadly lies and prejudices. It is based on wickedness, selfishness, racism, eugenics, imperialism, slavery, superiority complex, arbitrariness, violence, intolerance, vanity, hate, greed. We will give moral and psychological education to both torturers and victims of covid-19. Let's analyze the negative feelings and emotions engendered by covid-19, that is to say the bad states of mind of the victims.

Discouragement

People are discouraged. This means that they have lost the life energy which is the essence of the mind. The courageous man is the individual who is filled with mental, moral or spiritual energy. He is strong, powerful and enduring. He does not shrink from difficulties. He is not a fugitive, a coward, a weakling. So he can overcome obstacles, overcome challenges and succeed in everything. He manifests a great triumphant will. On the contrary, the discouraged man is weak, without will, without strength, without energy. He is defeated. He is someone who has given up the fight for life. He is depressed and pitiful. He has no value. He is without merit. Discouragement is a source of defeat and a serious illness that can completely cripple a man's life. It is to be fought. Rather, the world needs courageous and healthy men to save it. As a rule, any bad state of mind poisons the body or has harmful effects on it. In this regard, the ancient Romans said in Latin: "Mens sana in corpore sano". It means: a healthy mind in a healthy body. In other words, the health of the body comes from the health of the mind. Or the health of the mind produces the health of the body. This means that a sick mind necessarily intoxicates the body it inhabits and also makes it sick.

Despair

Despair is the loss of hope. A desperate man is one who has lost hope, who is afflicted, who has lost the taste for life or who expects nothing from life and the world. Despair is disappointment taken to the extreme with something or someone, the world or life in general. It is an extreme discouragement which can push someone to suicide, to death. It is a state of mental disorder that causes the individual to surrender, to give up everything and to let go of the worst. So despair is a catastrophic spiritual disease. Hope gives life and saves while despair kills. We must hope and believe in happiness, in the future, in a better tomorrow to build. Everything is done in the mind. We must always be optimistic and absolutely avoid rubbing shoulders with pessimism which leads to despair. You have to know how to reason with yourself and eliminate all your depressing and deadly thoughts, feelings and emotions. You have to learn to love your neighbor more than yourself. One must be indulgent, tolerant, affectionate, altruistic, non-selfish, compassionate, renouncing. Mens sana in corpore sano (a healthy body in a healthy mind).

Wickedness

Wickedness is the character of a wicked person. A wicked person is one who hurts, who harms others. It can attack their physical body, their life, their property, their interests etc. The wicked man is a danger to others and to himself. Indeed, the wicked can be condemned and punished by men, by the justice of men but above all by the natural, universal and cosmic order that he has disturbed. The bad guy is in the big Whole. He is an integral and inseparable part of this great Whole which always wants to be coherent, balanced and harmonious. When he poses an act harmful to this great Whole which constitutes him, he attacks himself directly by ignorance. He poisons himself like a drop of the ocean poisoning the whole ocean of which it is a part. This is insane and stupid, isn't it? Very stupid. It's suicide.

Any evil that man does against his neighbor necessarily turns against himself. Because he depends on the latter and is part of him. All people and all things live in a relationship of mutual interaction and interdependence. So if someone poisons the water he drinks, he kills himself. If he poisons the air he breathes, he kills himself. If he destroys all the plants or herbs on which his life depends (food, clothing, medicine, oxygen, house, shade, shelter etc.), he kills himself. If he spoils or destroys all his relationships with humans, with society, with his profession etc. that keep him alive, he condemns himself to suffering, poverty, misery, misfortune and death. Man has nothing and is nothing without the contribution and help of others, without solidarity, cooperation with others, without his harmonious integration into the great Whole. So every wicked act is a secession from the great Whole, a dissent and a fatal case of indiscipline worth a suicide.

Personal health is defined as a state of physical well-being, resulting from the balance and harmony that exist within oneself and in our relationships with others. If this condition is disturbed or suppressed, it follows physical or mental illness which leads to death. Let us all practice love of neighbor, kindness, generosity, compassion, altruism, self-giving, affection, tenderness, non-selfishness, renunciation or abandonment in order to live happy, in peace and in security.

Melancholy and sadness

Melancholy and sadness are two states of mind caused by discontent, frustration, suffering, pain and unhappiness. Melancholy manifests itself in depression and obsession with death and frequently accompanied by thoughts of suicide. Melancholy is deep, prolonged and catastrophic sadness. Unlike melancholy, sadness is a more or less lasting state of mind, which consists of a terrible feeling of dissatisfaction. Both are mental illnesses or psychic disorders that must absolutely be avoided. Because their consequences are disastrous for their subjects and for other men.

These two mental states ruin physical or spiritual health and destroy life. They therefore cause enormous losses. In order not to catch these two diseases, it is advisable to reason very well in the face of all the difficulties, all the situations and all the annoyances and to practice love of neighbor, kindness, indulgence, generosity, altruism, compassion, total renunciation, non-selfishness. We must fight egocentrism, pride and vanity.

Loss of taste for life

The loss of taste for life is the state of mind of one who no longer finds interest, joy, pleasure in living. Sometimes people get tired and disgusted with life. These people can no longer endure life. They no longer accept life. They no longer find meaning, reason for the life they lead. Life appears to them ugly, dirty, disgusting, awful, dangerous, harmful and worthless. These people despise, insult and condemn life. They then decide to leave it either spiritually (ascetics, religious, mystics, renunciators wandering in nature) or physically. They have the evil to live or the evil to be. They don't like life. They hate it.

This is the characteristic of people who are weak in character or in spirit, intoxicated and made sick. These include desperate, disappointed, disgruntled and discouraged people. These people should know that life is still beautiful, sweet and magnificent, despite corona virus. It is enough only to take it on the good side, to live it positively to be satisfied, happy and saved. Life is life. It's up to us to shape it to our liking and to always be calm, disciplined and positive towards it. Nothing is worth more than life. The salutary attitude here, as elsewhere, is love of neighbor, affection, tenderness, kindness, tolerance, indulgence, forgiveness, renunciation or abandonment.

Disappointment and worry

Disappointment is "the state of mind provoked by an event which reduces hope to nothing" (Jean Girodet). As for worry, it is "the state of a preoccupied, restless mind" (Jean Girodet). The disappointed man and the worried man are sick. They are both in danger. The disappointed man has lost hope. He is desesperate. It is very serious because he is disturbed and mentally imbalanced. His inner harmony and serenity are destroyed. He who is anxious is inhabited by fear and doubt. His fate is critical. He lives in disorder and suffering which are sources of unhappiness. The golden rule of health, happiness and salvation requires that one is out of these harmful states and that one is always and everywhere serene, balanced and in harmony with oneself and with the whole world. We must therefore cultivate love of neighbor, inner peace, compassion, altruism, non-egoism, tolerance, indulgence, affection, self-giving, salutary renunciation and abandonment.

Intolerance and fanaticism

Intolerance is "the persecuting hatred of those who believe they have the truth against those who do not have the same faith or the same opinions" (Jean Girodet). As for fanaticism, it is "blind and excessive zeal brought into the defense of a religion, a doctrine, a cause" (Jean Girodet). These two states of mind are very dangerous. They are very harmful because they consist of hatred, persecution, massacre, malfeasance. Intolerant or fanatic people want to dominate, subjugate others or, failing that, kill them, eliminate them. They are bad faith and mean. They are found in politics and religion. They want to impose their thoughts and practices on the whole world. So they cause wars and create conflicts everywhere. Against murderous intolerance and fanaticism, one should rather practice peaceful tolerance, indulgence, compassion, love, affection, kindness, non-egoism, altruism and renunciation or healthy abandonment.

Anguish and anxiety

Anguish and anxiety are vivid and oppressive emotions, worries. They are states or ways of being of a mind which is violently shaken, disturbed, agitated. It is the deprivation or the total absence of stillness, peace, serenity, tranquility, rest for the mind or soul of a person. The anguished or the anxious is someone who is very worried, very fearful in front of an important event.

Anxiety is a painful state which sometimes result in a prolonged tightness in the throat and general worry, whether there is a real danger or not. These conditions can cause death by causing cardiac arrest. We must therefore avoid them at all costs and remain calm in all situations. With very good reasoning, we can do it.

Rage and anger

Rage is a "violent movement of anger, of irritation" (Larousse). Anger is discontent accompanied by violent reactions. It is a "feeling, a state of irritation and aggression towards a being or something that hurts us, makes us unhappy." It is indignation against evil "(Jean Girodet). Rage and anger lead to harm to others and to oneself. Their consequences are very serious and painful. The harm you do to others turns against you. You pay it a hundredfold. In the state of rage, we totally lose control of ourselve and Reason (the sense of proportion, serenity, coolness, lucidity, discernment). We become crazy, stupid, nasty. We no longer own each other.

Someone who loses his temper frequently is in danger of death. He is exposed to fatal cardiovascular attacks. He is their easy prey. So let's absolutely avoid getting carried away in the face of everyday situations that upset us. To do this, let us practice the virtues of goodness, love of neighbor, altruism, compassion, indulgence, forgiveness, kindness, generosity, non-selfishness, salutary renunciation and abandonment.

Hate and aversion

Hate is the opposite of love, affection, compassion, kindness, tenderness, generosity, friendship and sympathy. It is a very harmful state of mind which manifests itself in a violent dislike or antipathy towards someone. The hateful individual is dangerous and mean. He wishes or causes misfortune to the man he hates. He wants to hurt him. He is willing to create trouble and pain for him. He is ruthless and cruel. Hatred generates conflicts between men, causes massacres, genocides, wars between peoples and nations.

Hatred destroys individual health, eats away and devastates the physical body. It produces cardiovascular attacks that kill the hater. We must fight hatred to preserve our health and protect our happiness. To do this, we must practice love of neighbor, kindness, generosity, affection, altruism, compassion, non-selfishness, renunciation or salutary surrender.

Resentment and the Spirit of Vengeance

Resentment is the state of mind of someone who feels hatred and deep resentment against his offender. The resentful man seeks revenge. Revenge consists in doing justice, that is to say in obtaining compensation or moral satisfaction by the punishment of the offender. The revenger is someone who does not want to forgive the offense of which he is the victim. He is not forgiving. He returns evil with evil, once for all. He practices the law of retaliation: "an eye for an eye, a tooth for a tooth, a bruise for a bruise" (Bible). He is nasty. And he is dangerous for himself and for the world. He establishes a law of infinite violence which can destroy everyone (the vendetta of Corsica).

You must always forgive and love your offender or enemy as yourself. Your neighbor is identical to you. He is you. You are him. In nature, the universe, the great Whole, all beings (men, animals, plants, minerals, air, water) are united, interdependent and in mutual interaction. Thus to harm one's neighbor is to harm oneself. This is why, it is good to do good to everyone, to practice the gift of oneself, non-egoism, altruism, kindness, love of neighbor, compassion, generosity, indulgence, forgiveness and healthy surrender.

Spite and resentment

Spite is a "Keeped memory of an offense and maintained with the intention of revenge" (Jean Girodet). It is a feeling of bitterness that one feels towards someone who is harmful with the resolution to punish or correct him. A spiteful or resentful man is a disgruntled person who does not want to forgive, who seeks revenge and hurts someone or who demands redress for a wrong, an injustice, a frustration etc. The grudge is an individual who does not forget and does not forgive the offenses or the inconveniences he has suffered from others. Grudge is resentment accompanied by the spirit of revenge. This spirit, or way of being, is nothing other than the desire for reparation or compensation. Right or wrong. The grudge can last as long as the grudge has not been compensated and satisfied. A resentful soul is a soul in pain, suffering, restless and disturbed soul. It is not at peace, serene, happy, quiet, secure.

Resentment is therefore a great danger, a great evil to be avoided for those who seek health, happiness, peace, serenity and salvation. Any imbalance, disorder and tension of soul is harmful to physical or physiological integrity of man. This gives more or less serious diseases to the body.

Animosity and hostility

Animosity and hostility are similar states of mind characterized by meanness, malevolence, a keen and persistent desire to harm someone. They manifest themselves as anger, antipathy, hatred, violence and aggression. Their opposites are benevolence, sympathy, gentleness, love, affection, kindness, compassion. A man hostile to another is dangerous for all others and for himself. He is not supportive, helpful, cooperative, sociable. His mind is toxic, unhealthy and evil. He is not in a relationship of peace, conviviality or fraternity with others. He is unlivable. Such a man is lonely and cannot be happy. Evil he does to others turns on himself and destroys him. Hostility and animosity make their perpetrators (those who practice them) very unhappy and kill them.

So no one has an interest in practicing them against his neighbor. It is love and kindness that save and make man happy. You have to learn to control your mind, to discipline it everywhere and at all times, in order to preserve your health and obtain your salvation.

Worry and fear

Worry is the lack of stillness, that is to say peace, serenity, calm in one's mind and soul. It is the turmoil and disturbance of soul and spirit based on the existence of misfortune or danger. Fear is the feeling that one experiences in the presence of real or possible danger. It is a feeling of worry and insecurity. Worry and fear are spiritual troubles. It is a disarray in the soul. A worried and fearful man is very unhappy. He lost his mental balance, the harmony within himself and his lucidity. He is troubled and broken.

If worry and / or fear persists in an individual and becomes chronic, it can lead to various physical ailments and diseases, the most serious of which are fatal cardiovascular attacks. So let's avoid panicking and trembling in the face of adversity, in front of the slightest difficulties, annoyances and everyday problems. Thus we will gain health and longevity.

Jealousy

Jealousy is a complex state of mind which manifests itself in the form of lust, envy, grief, selfishness and hatred for someone. It is the "passionate will to acquire or keep for oneself an advantage, a privilege" (Jean Girodet). Jealousy is therefore very dangerous. It is a host of mental illnesses or catastrophic dangers for the jealous himself and for his neighbor. Because all the constituents of jealousy are harmful or destructive. Hatred, lust, envy and selfishness make man suffer and make him very unhappy. A jealous man cannot control and own himself. He lost the serenity of his mind and the mastery of his soul. He is mentally unbalanced and broken. He is dangerous. So he hurts others. However, any harm that we do to others turns against us. Indeed, all beings (things, animals, men, plants etc.) are interdependent, in mutual interaction, intimately united and integrated into the great Whole that is the world, the universe or the cosmos. The laws which govern this great Whole and which ensure its conservation and security are love, harmony, balance, good, order, discipline, wisdom, prudence, solidarity, compassion, altruism, affection, kindness, generosity, non-selfishness, renunciation or abandonment. This is what ensures health, happiness and salvation of each and every one. The ignorant and the fool who try to destroy this harmony, this balance, this order, this universal beauty and good will be struck, punished and reduced to nothing. Rather, each of us has interest in working and collaborating in maintaining, preserving, securing, rescuing universal consistency and peace, this great happiness and this great good that is the great Whole. This is like an ocean of which each of us is a drop. And what is expected of this drop is that it behaves well towards the whole ocean, that it is very disciplined not to poison the whole ocean and therefore itself.

Conclusion

Covid-19 is demystified. **He is overcome by philocure**. It is now up to each person to apply philocure, to move away resolutely from the false fear (unfounded, unjustified fear) of suicide and to no longer believe in the **global lie** represented by covid-19. It is imperative that everyone get rid of this ghost, this crushing and deadly burden that is covid-19. Time must be for mental and psychological resistance. Everyone must strengthen his soul, his spirit. Let us be everywhere and always serene. Let us believe and know that this lie cannot and must not take our lives. Let us fight with boldness and intrepidity against the propagators of this lie (their business assets and their political ideology). We have to face the globalists, the eugenics, the capitalist imperialists, the Malthusians, the Utopians, the Illuminati, the Freemasons and the Satanists. We must fight, to their last entrenchment, the murderers of mankind who want to depopulate earth with sterilizing and deadly vaccinations, with toxic gases, bacteriological and chemical attacks, by climate modification, air pollution (carbon dioxide sulfur hydrogen sulfate covid), by geoengineering. Let us reject the new world order of madmen, cynics, sadists and criminals who rule earth in the shadows.

Karl Marx taught us the duality of classes, that is to say the struggle between the bourgeoisie and the proletariat. Under his instigation, the proletariat won this struggle. Today we have unions and workers'associations all over the world defending workers' rights. Everything is not yet perfect on earth with regard to the socio-economic question and labor legislation. However, a great step has been taken. There is relative progress or some improvement in the lot of workers around the world. Humanity is no longer quite at the time of slavery, feudalism or the bourgeoisie one hundred percent. Today there is also socialism and communism. It is an appreciable achievement thanks to Marxism-Leninism. Well-being, comfort, happiness, security, justice, peace and dignity are things now shared with everyone.

But hardly out of this war or class duality, humanity finds itself grappling with a harsher war. It is no longer a duality this time but a **triality** or **triangularity**. The world is made up of a human triangle. This is a fierce conflict that takes place between three groups of people around the world (executioners, slaves and rebels) hence the idea of the human triangle. This is precisely the globalists or creators of a new world order, their victims (or 80% of the world population they want to kill) and those who are trying to resist them (the rebels). This is the new deal in history or the new dynamic in the world. This new war is raging all over earth. People die in disorder every day, sprayed like cockroaches by the globalists (spraying, drugs, vaccinations, toxic foods, 5 G, climate change...). People are confined to their homes, deprived of their liberty, of work, of leisure, of pleasure, of movement, of meeting, muzzled, masked, starving, sick, murdered in hospitals. It is the most terrible general, universal catastrophe ever known in history. It is general distress and panic everywhere.

If the proletarians have won their war against the bourgeoisie, can we hope one day to see the victory of the slaves and the rebels over the executioners, their common enemies? Whoever wrestles will be saved. He will be saved by his struggle. Victory will come from the sacrifices made by all the victims of the new world order, from the resolute and unreserved commitment of all the peoples of earth who are targeted and condemned to be killed by the globalist eugenics. To be able to wager a fight or a war, it is necessary to attack the enemy without respite and not to flee from him. You who read this book, define yourself. Determine yourself. Who exactly are you? Executioner, slave or rebel? **We want everyone to be rebel.** Let us together create the Universal Community of Rebels for the salvation of all of us. Let's all turn into rebels. The sacred and revolutionary union of the rebels or death. We will vanquish!

Book Summary

Today's world is made up of executioners, slaves and rebels. It is a "triality" or "triangularity". The executioners are like lions. They devour all the weak (slaves and rebels). They destroy the world. What to do in the face of this supreme danger ? Let us all turn into rebels to save humanity and earth. Let us resist the globalists, the eugenics, the executioners and their new satanic, infernal world order. Let us defeat all their evil plans and plots. It is a question of life or death. There is no other choice.

Author's Biography

Dr. François Adja Assemien was born on March 15, 1954 in Côte d'Ivoire (West/Africa). He studied the humanities (Latin, Greek), the social sciences and philosophy. He is graduate in philosophy (Ph.D.) and in sociology (Bachelor's degree). He devoted himself to teaching (philosophy), writing and academic research. He speaks and writes three modern languages: French, English and German.

He is author of several works published in Europe and the United States of America (novels, essays, short stories, plays) and of several concepts such as Afrocratism, Philocure, Sidarology, African consciousness, Philosophy of African spirit, Aboubou music. He is also an artist, musician, composer, singer and guitarist. He lives in the United States of America.

www.ingramcontent.com/pod-product-compliance
Lightning Source LLC
LaVergne TN
LVHW041550060526
838200LV00037B/1220